MW01119384

imagination series # 9

Metropolis Burning

Karen Kovacik

Cleveland State University Poetry Center

Metropolis Burning

Acknowledgments

My thanks to the editors of the following magazines, first publishers of these poems:

Artful Dodge: "During the Sorties over Baghdad"
Crab Orchard Review: "Blue Paris," "Church of St. James, Warsaw, Ochota District / W kościele Św. Jakuba, Warszawa Ochota," "From *The Indianapolis City Directory,* 1916: A Tally"
Glimmer Train Stories: "Songs for a Belgrade Baker"
Green Mountains Review: "The Story of My Life, As Written by My Mother"
GSU Review: "Miami Sands Motel, 1958"
Indiana Review: "Portrait of the Poet as an Exchange Student, 1986" [as "Self-Portrait in Warsaw, With My Least Favorite Color"]
Laurel Review: "Breslau"
Maize: "Chernobyl Diary," "Parting / Parturition"
Massachusetts Review: "To Warsaw"
Meridian: "Jankowice, Poland," "Litany"
Mudfish: "If my grandfather had not emigrated from Silesia"
Nimrod: "Ultrasound"
Sycamore Review: "Poem for My Journal That Disappeared"
Visions International: "History of a Heel and Its Mate," "Versions of Irena"
West Branch: "My Mother the Monopolist," "Return to the Mother Tongue"

"Little Pigeons" appeared in the anthology *And Know This Place: Poetry of Indiana* (Indiana University Press, 2005). "Requiem for the Buddhas of Bamiyan" won the 2002 Barbara Mandigo Kelly Peace Poetry Prize, awarded by the Nuclear Age Peace Foundation. It was originally published on the website www.wagingpeace.org and then in the anthology, *The Poetry of Peace* (NAPF, 2003). "During the Sorties over Baghdad" and "Breslau" also appeared in *Beyond the Velvet Curtain,* winner of the Stan and Tom Wick Poetry Prize (Kent, OH: Kent State University Press, 1999).

I would like to thank Indiana University Purdue University Indianapolis for two summer travel grants that aided in the writing of these poems and the Arts Council of Indianapolis for a Creative Renewal Fellowship.

And thanks to the Irregular Sundays Writing Group (Alice, Barb, Bonnie, Catherine, Elizabeth K, and Elizabeth W) for their invaluable revision suggestions and delicious eats. This book would not have been possible without the wise counsel and creative passion of Cathleen, Eduardo, Ellen, Eric, Jim, Joanna, Linda, Marge, Marilyn, Missy, Susan G, Susan S, and Terry. Finally, to Maggie Anderson, David Citino, Sam Hazo, Jesse Lee Kercheval, Ron Wallace, and Carolyne Wright: hugs and admiration and gratitude.

Published by Cleveland State University Poetry Center
Department of English
2121 Euclid Avenue
Cleveland, OH 44115-2214
ISBN: 1-880834-66-9
Library of Congress Catalog
Card Number: 2005921327

Ohio Arts Council

A STATE AGENCY THAT SUPPORTS
PUBLIC PROGRAMS
IN THE ARTS 40 Years

Contents

The Art of Poetry   1

1   Warsaw

To Warsaw   5
Church of St. James, Warsaw, Ochota District /
        W kościele Św. Jakuba, Warszawa Ochota   6
Warsaw Architect   7
Chernobyl Diary   8
Litany   10
From *The Book of Polish Men*: Farce   11
A Closed Concert   12

2   Origins

If my grandfather had not emigrated from Silesia   15
From *The Book of Polish Men*: Fable   16
Jankowice, Poland   17
Versions of Irena   18
Little Pigeons   20
Miami Sands Motel, 1958   22
History of a Heel and Its Mate   23
Liquid Syntax   24
The Story of My Life, As Written by My Mother   26
My Mother the Monopolist   27
Poem for My Journal That Disappeared   28
Portrait of the Poet as an Exchange Student, 1986   30
Return to the Mother Tongue
        (After a Month of Polish)   32
Parting / Parturition   33
Song to Saint Ambrose   34

3   Atlas

   Ultrasound   39
   Blue Paris   40
   From *The Indianapolis City Directory*, 1916: A Tally   41
   In Medias Res x 5   42
   Breslau   44
   Imagining Walter Benjamin, 1939   46
   Woman at Streetcar Stop   47
   During the Sorties over Baghdad   48
   Meditation at the Gästehaus Mezcalero, Dresden   49
   Requiem for the Buddhas of Bamiyan   50
   Songs for a Belgrade Baker   52

   Notes   54

for Pete and Fran Kovacik

I was a boatman on the Nile. . . then Greek rhetorician in Suburra, where I was devoured by bedbugs. I died, during the Crusades, from eating too many grapes on the beach in Syria. I was pirate and monk, mountebank and coachman . . . .

—Gustave Flaubert

The Art of Poetry

Like a cradle or an open valise
it bobbed toward the Cleveland shore—
camelback velveted with wine brocade,
two oval stones resting on its lap—
this sofa red as Rousseau's, something a naked woman
might ride when facing oncoming tigers.

From which dock, from whose boat
did its bottom salute the waves?
Why abandon a blood-colored davenport
in the lake? I hoped no well-off aunt
had been dispatched on the couch after lunch,
no lover smothered on that plush valentine.

Perhaps the couch belonged to cousins
too poor to afford the dump.
After four decades in the parlor
and two on the porch, its horsehair
succumbed to mice, and its rough springs
troubled even the stoutest guest.

"Notice what you notice," said Allen Ginsberg.
Cleveland believes in onion domes and boxcars.
Lake Erie is no sea of angelfish and sharks.
Its wildlife runs to glass, bricks from a wayward kiln,
and the occasional upholstered divan.
Poetic justice: when image fits idea like a workboot.

Wake sofa, I still see you swaying: hallucination,
cartoon refugee from an attic of doilies and holy cards.
In second grade, they pronounced Lake Erie dead.
Now zebra mussels and poetry have brought it back:
gray silk to drape over furniture,
wet music to launch this unlikely boat.

1 *Warsaw*

I built on the sand
And it tumbled down,
I built on a rock
And it tumbled down.
Now when I build, I shall begin
With the smoke from the chimney.

—Leopold Staff

To Warsaw

Your Kino Moscow gleams like a pink dish
with the films of Clint Eastwood and French farce.

I feel like an umbrella in for repair.
I'd rather be a telescope, to see past
the scrim of things American,
to smell past pickles, smoke, and grief
and understand the idiom of uprisings.

You are the map that exists and the ones that have disappeared.
You are the cigarette that makes the slow bus come.

I'm a thin glass of oolong, lucky in lust,
in this province of lip and teeth
where syllables squeak like sugar
and our hands are always hot
and my marriage dies on double beds of cake.

You are a museum of ailing clocks,
you are streets named Barley, Gold, and Starch.

I watch a man on a train eat a tomato
like an apple. He keeps checking his pockets
for spies. Why so nervous? I wonder.
He licks his fingers and whispers:
"The Jews, they're everywhere."

You are the church and the candles in the church,
the bank and the money, the book and the words.

I avoid talk. My bangs are trimmed
by the centimeter. The hives look like dollhouses
and Józek feeds me raw honey.
Although I'm afraid, I watch and taste.
I have few words, but will tell of it.

Church of St. James, Warsaw, Ochota District / W kościele Św. Jakuba, Warszawa Ochota

The frescoes are burning, in sunlight and in gloom,
at Sunday Mass or with a single widow praying,
because they were painted with a tindery hand,
because the fingers that held the brush knew pleasure,
knew where to touch, for how long, with what pressure,
and there was no need to call his beloved "beloved"
because she saw the rich arterial reds of her body,
the umber of brow and belly, transmuted
in the suffering of saints. Didn't she pose
as Joan? Didn't she writhe against a drape
of purple? Didn't the blaze scorch her calves, her thighs,
hot on the bowl of her hips, her unchaste breasts?
And when the flames touched her throat,
there was no color for her keening, so the painter
chose restraint, elongation, the ecstatic silence
of Peter hanging naked on an inverted cross
or Paul suffering lightning bolts to the eyes.
This painter was no stranger to illumination,
to doves big as owls descending, to virgins
gazing at angels armed with swords of love.
He had seen the capital desolate, all habitation
forsaken, loose horses wandering the avenues
as in a wilderness. This painter had smelled dynamite
and hid in sewers, discovered a talent for small acts
of sabotage and once rescued a stranger's piano.
Later, there was nothing to do but mix bloody colors
in the unaccustomed calm. Later, there was no need
to paint devils because eleven fresh apostles
had risen from the palette of hell. These frescoes are burning,
and I'm listening to their silence:
speak, you flame-tongued supplicants and martyrs,
O speak, evangelists of shrapnel and of wax.

Warsaw Architect

Let there be modernism, he says, and in the radiant flat world
arising on his square of bristol, a cube shimmers.
Then balconies appear, and freshly waxed floors, and kitchens
still innocent of grease and smoke. Will he add
some tall cones of cedar or a brush tip of poplar?
Anything is possible beneath the thin gouache sky.

His own apartment is a wreck of central planning:
low ceilings, cracked tile, the orange linoleum
of some Seventies' utopia. Exposed wires
dangle in the hall, the lift reeks of garbage.
A Freudian billboard obscures the house number
with praise for a cigarette "both strong and hard."

How does he move between these realms?
What passport of intellect or spirit allows him
to forsake parabola and grid for this corridor
weeping with onions? On his screen,
Warsaw appears flat as paper, a page erased by fire,
before granite dreams of coalminers holding up the world.

Outside a cold rain, chimneys and pavement
the color of tea, women hauling in stockings
from the balconies. I love the hand's provisional flourish,
before the first line, when anything can emerge—
even this Austrian market with suburban shoppers,
even this highrise of breakfast flakes, this Danube of soda.

Chernobyl Diary

The morning express from Gdańsk brakes in Warsaw Central Station, and travelers in wrinkled skirts and stiff Soviet jeans, some half asleep and others nervous to start the day, gather up their belongings.

My husband slides our bags from a metal shelf, I grab his hooded poncho from a hook. To evade pickpockets, we synchronize our movements without any English.

Returning home to Warsaw makes me glad because no one stares at me there; nothing in my clothes or haircut, not even my full set of teeth, seems exotic in the capital.

This is a Tuesday. Our flat opens onto a courtyard with mature poplars. On parallel iron bars that a gymnast might use, a woman is beating her rugs.

This is an April of open windows after a winter of dusk at 3. This April smells like river mud and the urine of our neighbor's 20 cats.

Under the satin featherbed's cool skin, we hesitate, about to make love, half-listening to the BBC, when Stockholm interrupts. A meteorologist reports high levels of cesium and strontium on Swedish soil.

Moscow, Gorbachev, the Ukrainian reactor still burning.

We crank shut the casement windows, call all our friends who have phones.

Outside, pensioners sit as usual on the steps of Castle Square, with their violets, pumice stones, garlic braids and steel wool arranged for sale on shiny Marlboro bags.

I bring home violets tied with butcher's string, but my husband doesn't want them in the house. We stop brewing coffee or tea and wet our toothbrushes with tonic water.

Sunshine, pear trees blooming, our windows looking south. Everything in Warsaw appears natural and pure except for the children leaving the cathedral, the O-gape of their mouths purpled with some violent grape.

Turns out that every *Apteka* has prescribed tincture of iodine. "Just one more sip," Ela is saying to seven-year-old Janek. "*Proszę Cię,* one more sip."

Litany

after A. R.

on Napoleon's field map
the site circled in black ink
Varsovie

beside the Hotel Bristol's poppy torte
or at Paderewski's last recital
Warszawa

stamped on the Semitic boy's diploma
on souvenir aprons stitched in blue thread
Warszawa

then in Gothic script on metal road signs
the unwelcome translation
Warschau

incised in Hebrew on a marble pillar
on every tramcar and trolley-bus
in the train tables of Europe

Warszawa Varsovie Warschau

above arcades in the Soviet style
spraypainted green by a soccer fan
Warszawa

on blue envelopes
with your address in my hand
Warsaw

this city of cherries in summer
smoked prunes in winter
city halved by the Vistula's gray knife

whether burning or rising
its syllables are stiff against my teeth
its name a coal on my tongue

From *The Book of Polish Men:* Farce

How does Charlie Chaplin become a dictator? How does a cobbler metamorphose into a soldier? Private Szymon Z, reporting! I'm here at the Warsaw Yacht Club, defending my city's fanciest boats against willows, dragonflies, and the treacherous sandbars of the Vistula.

At the end of each August afternoon, I mark a red X on the calendar just as I used to after days of replacing soles. I wonder what genius dreamed up these official-issue black lace-ups, which are choking my toes and cratering my heels. You'll know the loser by his boots.

What I wouldn't give for a smoke. A mogul's cigar. Even one of those limp handrolled jobs by Wanda or Ania at The Red Parrot.

> *So to her I say,*
> *"Dear Madam, s'il vous plait,*
> *My flat is right this way,"*
> *But she winces like I'm poison.*
> *"Sir, you are too crass,*
> *Too modern and too fast,*
> *Kindly let me pass,"*
> *And she blew a ring of cigarette smoke.*

What I wouldn't give.

But what's this? A uniformed officer of high rank boarding one of the yachts. Stiff-looking, old-fashioned, wearing a monocle of all things. Arm extended in what appears to be a Nazi salute. Heil Hitler? Hell no, you fool! This colonel is reaching for the gloved hand of a woman half his age, if this ridiculous spyglass can show me anything. Seamed stockings, a high instep, and a T-strap pump in white, probably last spring's Easter shoe. No slip as far as I can tell.

He's undoing the buckle of her right shoe. This is one man of the sword who understands the erotics of the ankle. A kiss to the instep! There he is reaching under the skirt to ease her ghostly stocking off. From the look on her face, all armaments have crossed the frontiers.

It's lucky I have them under surveillance. . .

A Closed Concert

He was a baritone.
In his tremolo, she could detect lost letters,
sexual fidelity, and his dead wife's cold kitchen
heated only once a week. Lithuanian medicinal plants
thrived in his voice as did extinct species of birds
and pig's legs weighed by the kilo.

She was a shake-her-ass soprano
who created a style of modernist scorchers.
Beguiling, seeking new pleasures, she heard
his memoirs from the ghetto and warmed them
with two octaves of pomegranate trees
and a nest of silver birch fire.

Bodily truths bloomed in their liturgies,
which they performed in their porcelain washtub
or beneath the leaky prewar eiderdown.
He offered fifty flavors of death, she the rallying
of heat and need. Their blended voices
banished cold, vanquished rue without tears.

2 *Origins*

Life began in the trough with a moist, throaty whisper,
and continued with soft kerosene song.

—Osip Mandelstam

If my grandfather had not emigrated from Silesia

I would have been born between Auschwitz and Krakow
My first vowels would've been nasal
my first consonants a grafting of whisper and cherry
The nearest city would be two blue buses away
but I wouldn't think of leaving
The uncles would teach me morels and red currants
The aunts would bottle yellow plums on a wood stove
and stew hens whose necks I had snapped with practiced hands
I would dream of sliced beets in their lovely fuchsia lake
I would pack a rabbit in my mother's purse
then at a neighbor's undo the clasp and up would pop
the checkered ears, the still, pink eye
At twelve, I would visit a dentist for the first time
The loud pain would make me cry
but afterwards my smile would be pretty and gold
A bible and 1940s album of Stalin
would be my only books
I would memorize that mustachioed face, poreless
as an actor's on a movie poster, eyes glassy
as my rabbit's, and fall asleep with the strange man's arms
open on the slippery pages
The city teachers would whisper about me
Blushing, I would struggle with their questions
posed in the quick, sharp tones of the capital
The other children would call me dunce, baboon
and after school, I would walk home alone
fast on the yellow days of fall, then later
slow over frozen mud, and at my lane
I'd salute the storks atop the lamp pole in their nest
brown and deep-brimmed as a fancy lady's hat

From *The Book of Polish Men:* Fable

I was the fourth son of poor parents but well brought up. One night, when I was nineteen I heard music. An accordion, some horns, and a metal drum. I walked down the lane, listening, till I came to the baker's house. The door was open—a wedding! I hung back because I was shy. And my family had not been invited. The uncle of my father was serving seven years for refusing to give up his rifles after the war.

The bridegroom caught me by the shoulder and pulled me to the kitchen. Before me was a beer mug long as my arm. Drink, he commanded. As soon as I did, he poured me another, foamy and dark as the last. Then he brought out a steaming round loaf and urged me to eat. I hesitated, not wanting to seem greedy. Eat, he bellowed. You'll dishonor me if you don't. I tore into the bread, burning my fingers. Next he gave me a loop of sausages, which I stuffed into my pockets when he reached into the icechest for vodka. Bottoms up, he ordered. After many minutes, I came up for air. Now it's time to dance, he said. But the one-two-three, one-two-three made the floor tilt. Besides, I was ashamed of my homemade shirt and trousers.

So I went outside and fell asleep under a tree. Late the next morning, I was still there, thirstier than I had ever been before or since. And that's when the miracle occurred: above my head hung hundreds of cherries, black with juice. I grabbed a branch, tipped the new fruit into my mouth. May the lonely, the lovesick, and the dying recover as I did that day—lying in the sun under those mercifully low branches, my ancient mother in the distance calling my name.

Jankowice, Poland

A black veil hangs from my hat: I am learning bees—
the incest, the swoop of them, their love
of tunnels, silky buzzing under blankets—
all this I want to learn because I am thirty
and restless and noticing the finch-colored
clothespins flying on the line or the sunflowers
six feet tall, coveted by the village elite
to hedge their stuccoed homes. I am thirty
and every inch of my body feels unloved
but awake, the electricity on but no glow
in my belly, in my bony arms, no lamplit
wings to thrust me over the cups of flowers
to sip their sweet milk. All this I grasp
from my uncle's coalmining hands,
his nails tiny shafts of ore, the palms educated
in sickle and drill, fingers that speak anthracite
or clover, that have been stung by a hundred bees
but survive to twirl my aunt on linoleum
then summon the small of my back out of stiffness,
sweet wheezing accordion in 3/4 time.
I'm the waltz, I'm the polka, I'm honey
still warm from the hive, loudness
that will not let him sleep, nectar-flavored
vodka on his capable tongue, and yes, friend,
a black veil hangs from my hat, but I am no widow:
I am learning bees.

Versions of Irena

for my aunt who grew up near Oświęcim [Auschwitz]

Chronology
When she was five, her great delight was gooseberry juice.
At seven, she experienced the strangeness of books.
When she was ten, her beloved uncle expired at the table.
At eleven, she refused to leave the coal stove in the corner.
By twelve, she had forgotten her uncle's bloody cough.
At thirteen, she chewed poppy leaves and hallucinated music.
When she turned fourteen, her dress grew tight in the bodice.
At fifteen, she scrubbed the parlor of a short Nazi sergeant,
        and the night smelled of cognac and smoke.
At twenty, her mind declared war on her body.
For years, local doctors have regarded her case with gravity.

1943
She could smell them burning, their forgotten
valises in a corner of the yard
along with topcoats and short pants, sheet music,
maps with foreign bodies of water,
a book of French pictures. She hid the brittle pages
in her coat. Midnight was the hour
of gravity, when the sergeant swung the bell
on his table. He wanted his heart's delight:
something milky to help him sleep, warmed cognac
to dull his dreams. Nights, she smelled them burning.

1986
Having lost her uterus at 25, she feels the effects
of gravity, her lumpy body without music or delight.
She walks plates of white bacon from the table
to the sink, and rinses the grease in cool suds.
Behind her sits the American niece with a short book

of Polish phrases. The girl hardly ate her supper
and only sweetened her tea with one sugar.
Time to slide the featherbed into the starched cover
and make up the girl's couch in the corner.
She wishes her niece untroubled dreams:
"What we've forgotten," she says, "will not harm us,
and only sleep can take the war out of night."

Little Pigeons

for Mary Kovacik, 1907-1968

Named for those messy birds,
those lilac roosting birds,
your balls of beef and pork
wrapped in cabbage lips
stink up the flat.

The kitchen is Pepto-Bismol pink,
square stomach with a leaky drain.
Your bathtub's on lion paws.
The ceiling's a pink slope. Your pantry
smells like sauerkraut and flax.

I know you by your city chicken.
I know your orange Supp-hose,
Pope Pius XII in cloak and dress
on your cedar chest,
chenille snowflakes on your bed.

Your nose is flat, Polish
vowels tighten the fat triangle of your chin.
I wish you were less a mystery.
I wish when you hum the rosary
your mother and father,

dead of influenza since 1918
would rise from the chattering sleep
of fever, into their world of umbrellas
and streetcar pennies and pince-nez.
You an orphan at 11

I know by your broad lap,
your housedress buttoned at the shoulder.

I know your cackle at parties,
your calendars of saints.
The butcher Adam, local genius

of veal cutlets, tempts us
with wands of pickle and pretzel.
I love your wire shopping cart,
your shuttered television,
the orange marshmallow peanuts

you pass out for treats.
I wish your stoic Peter,
stoop-shouldered at 39,
would have outlasted U.S. Gypsum.
What did it cost you to nurse

his stomach tumor in your kitchen?
Did you cough your grief
into a hankie of crochet?
Did you never speak of it?
Did you dominate the card table,

full-fleshed, over butterscotch cake?
Little pigeon, little dove,
long these years vanishing,
I know your ripe cabbage rolls,
your coils of poppyseed.

I wish you were less a mystery.

Miami Sands Motel, 1958

No one told her he would bite her shoulder,
or that red rosettes would bloom on his chest.
How remote this was from Sister Belane's
lesson about periods, the sacraments
of sperm and egg. She never imagined
the bed would gallop from the wall, or starched
topsheet and spread would slither to the rug.
The old nun had not mentioned greed, never
hinted that he'd hoist up on an elbow,
opening the long scissors of her legs
with his knee, and tell her he wanted to
"taste" her. Yes, his teeth looked carnivorous
in the bedside light as they never had
in his Rambler or her mother's kitchen,
though what she sensed was soft and warm, not sharp,
his applying of polish to a part
she had never thought to touch. She felt like
a marble dropped in a pond, sinking deep
in the fizzy rush till all signs of land—
green neon through Venetian blinds, champagne
on ice, shelf with her white cosmetic case—
vanished in the wake. For she was drifting
to some peninsula where people spoke
in sighs, her body now a pink F sharp
unspooling from his breath and tongue and hands.

History of a Heel and Its Mate

Mother Hubbard couldn't live in this high-rise,
this red leather vamp with three-inch heel
and skinny ankle strap. Birthed on a metal last
in Saõ Paulo, this *sapato* limped
down the assembly line till it was fished
from the dyer's vat, bloody as a lipstick.
The cutter and stitcher took two brief breaks
for *cafezinho* and another for *lanche*.
Fifty cents an hour went into these shoes,
and the tanned and trimmed skin of a calf.

Her husband had purchased the pair in Florida,
tipping the salesboy extra to surprise her
when she asked for a navy pump.
Admiring the scarlet tip and throat, fitting her palm
to the foxing, she allowed the silver horn
to spoon her 7AA into the severe, angled arch,
watched him tighten the ankle strap,
then glided into a cha cha before the prim floor mirror.

And the rest, as they say, is history:
how the shoe slept with its mate in pink tissue.
How she lavished toe and heel with polish.
How, five years later, mid-rhumba,
she collapsed on the varnished floor
in a crash of underskirts and silk.
And after Mt. Sinai failed to revive her,
her husband, in the ambulance, sped home,
stunned at the heft of her red pocketbook,
the airy loft of her matching shoes.

Liquid Syntax

Before labor or shame or the beloved's kiss
the wish to postpone arrival
the desire to be lost
begins in a wild box of crayons
when the child writes R A I N
in her drugstore calendar
and out the window
real silver is falling
and the word on the page
is more than the hinge and hook
of pressure on wax
the letters shooting open like parasols
or maples in slow motion
the calendar pages
March April May
dissolving into a city
the child has not yet seen
but she can smell its wet wool
its boulevards of neon and chocolate
the hexagons of sidewalk
that invite her in
and though her mother is cooking
veal pocket and green beans
maraschino tapioca for dessert
the child has booked a room
for the evening
in the letter R
where from its window
she watches the bracelet of lights
sway along the river
and beneath her sloping ceiling
beneath the roof of staccato rain
she undresses whole sentences
like paper dolls

or the sheet music for "Volga Boatman"
each letter like a piano key
which is not pure sound
not the world
but a button she can press
to make the world appear
turning TANG into TANGO
RIG into RIGOR
and though she can't foresee it
out of a tunnel of reverses
she will aim for the dazzle
of what her English will allow
its boroughs now her boroughs
with their intricate streets
its river the one she will fish in
beads of rain lighting the way overhead

The Story of My Life, As Written by My Mother

Yes, she played with the neighborhood kids,
but hated Duck Duck Goose and Tag.
She preferred Cemetery there on the front lawn,
a green towel covering her body with an index card:
KAREN KOVACIK, 1959-1967.

Her favorite mysteries of the rosary
were the sorrowful. Loved scaring her younger sister
by pretending to scourge Christ at the pillar,
all fangs and whip. Had a stuffed pig named Snoozy Q,
which, according to her, changed sex twice a day.

I should have seen the signs, I know:
the eighth grade girls despising her
for using words like "ingenue" and "corpulent,"
the notebooks she kept on high school dates.
College only made her worse. At supper it became,

"As Byron once said," or "John Donne put it best. . ."
Now she was a quote-unquote intellectual wearing men's hats
and toreador pants purchased at Goodwill.
"Where did I go wrong?" I once asked her.
"Not believing in birth control?" she replied.

Now, God forbid, she has started to publish.
For years, I've dreaded the day, have woken in the night,
shaking and sad, imagining a life of betrayals.
She doesn't offer to show, and I don't ask. Better to imagine
she hasn't written anything too mean about us. Yet.

My Mother the Monopolist

Thimble
Queen of the needle, she always chose this tiny
silver silo as her token. Emblem of thrift,
no prodigal, it tap-tapped at even the swankest
addresses. She embroidered pillowcases with tulips
while she waited for my brother to get out of jail.

Utilities
Her nightmare: a world without plumbing or light.
The first on the block to get a dishwasher,
she seized control of every faucet, every bulb,
and rapped her steel pinkie in triumph
when our rates went through the roof.

B & O
She smelled of Jean Naté bath salts and Russian musk,
maybe VO5 setting lotion or Dippity-Do.
Never Bacon & Onion, never Barnyard & Offal.
Yet she championed this reeking iron beast
that flattened our billfolds each time it crossed us.

Baltic Avenue
Forget Park Place, Boardwalk, or the luxury tax.
She always acquired the tawdry purple street
no one else wanted. Lovingly, she furnished it
with squat green bungalows and cheap hotels.
Many a red night, Dad blew his paycheck there.

Chance
When question marks assailed her like boomerangs,
she simply built more skyscrapers of pastel cash.
This was her metropolis: the sun a fluorescent ring
on plaster sky, while chili sweated on the stove.
She fanned herself with fifties, cool and blue.

Poem for My Journal That Disappeared

I lost all of June and half-July.
A slice of summer, orange-red
with blue wires humming
on every page: my notebook.
Unfinished poems fell still
in its interior, caught
mid-leap like fish,
pink and ghostly blue,
before the slow descent
into breath. In one poem
it's 1965, a peach kitchen
where my aunt cans pickles
in a storm of alum and sweat.
In another, my friend
cries into a dishtowel
at her teenaged daughter's wake—
beside the pewter urn,
the girl's creased paperback
of *Das Kapital*—
while outside, kids loop
through the dark with sparklers,
pretending to be lightning bugs.
I lost a month of weather,
the moon cycling through
its changes, a month of hormones
and psalms. Gemini
gave way to Cancer,
the spokes of my bike wheels
spun finite revolutions,
wands of rhubarb simmered
with sugar on the range
before they turned into pie.
My notebook vanished

in a library—claimed by a snoop,
slipped from my bag—
who knows? It fell
in a forest of words,
and I didn't hear.

Portrait of the Poet as an Exchange Student, 1986

Warsaw was the earnest newsreel
that everyone talked through.
Warsaw was sexy train tunnels
and 40-watt streets.
On New World Avenue,
I hunched in milk bars
like a double agent
and swilled brackish soups
of cucumber or kapusta,
then washed down a sour avalanche of rye
with compote sloshing
its saucer like dishwater.

I coughed imperfect verbs
on my fingers, while matrons
in prewar silver minks
elbowed past me onto tramcars.
I stole slices of window
and watched the world turn
to limestone. Stalin wanted Warsaw
full of ten-foot hunks:
steelworkers and miners
with dreamy granite eyes
aimed at a socialist future.
Forget neon Hollywood
and its stupid rosy tints!

Warsaw lurked in the backseats
of cabs and smoky salons
where poets with gray matter,
prematurely gray,
kissed me in every dialect
of tobacco and rewired
my accusative and dative.

Warsaw was silver Wyborowa
whose caps I could never unscrew
fast enough. Virile plurals
and feminine endings.

A city of lavender pigeons
strutting for new mates.
City of aphrodisiac kasha
and noirish eel.
City I still struggle to capture
in charcoal. Whose churches
I can never make pregnant.

Return to the Mother Tongue
(After a Month of Polish)

I'm back in my language, beyond the gilt
deckle of the kingsize dictionary,
past "May I?" and "Please." I've cast off the silk
muzzle of sibilants, stopped rationing
words like rosary beads or martyring
myself on unforgiving verbs. I'm through
with ankle-length dresses, averted eyes.
I'm back to demanding, my tongue a burr
instead of a velvet-tipped begonia,
I'm back to bitchiness and bravado,
no sin or syntax too abstruse. So what
if I belch adjectives or spill nouns down
the front of my dress? I'm back to shooting
straight, cutting up, letting prepositions
fizz up over my glass to be savored
by my naked tongue. I'm back in English,
language that could never keep a budget,
language with a straining waistband, lover
of karaoke, maracas and borscht.
I'm back in Chicago, hallelujah!
Now I will talk *you* under the table,
now *I* will decide how long and how hard.

Parting / Parturition

            Amniotic this love
that has been our element:
            airless, lightless,
with only a varicose music,
            it's the wet blanket
we try to kick
            off in sleep,
our blue vestigial fists
            impenitent.

Grief is the gravy
            we breathe. Grief is
our mothers' kitchens,
            the one-star restaurants
we can't stop frequenting
            where we doze, spent,
then wake to the gray TVs
            that cleave us.

Now comes the eviction,
            my bearded twin.
It's vascular, embossed
            in red and blue
like a deed. All efforts
            to barricade us in
are futile. Soon

            we'll be hurled
down a chute
            into alien arms
or light's unexpected wreath
            or a happiness so sharp
we think it's death.

Song to Saint Ambrose

Born in Milan in 340,
patron of beekeepers and candlemakers,
you stand before me in wood,
your bishop's crook and mitre,
even the bags beneath your eyes
the color of honey.
My uncle carved you in July
in this Polish village
from the trunk of a linden,
the radio his only choir,
news from distant capitals
guiding his diabetic fingers
stained with tobacco and sap.
Washington London Berlin Moscow
each inflected his chisel,
furrowing the folds in your robe,
your pouched eyes now resembling his eyes
swollen from suffering, yet calm.
And when you stood
in honeyed, idiosyncratic splendor
he anointed you with resin
so you would glow even in winter
even when a rook perched on your mitre,
when bees swarming from their gumball-colored hives
engulfed you in their fury.
You live now in a village of hives,
one shaped like a Polynesian hut,
another an onion-domed church,
still others petite gabled houses,
their pitched roofs shaded by pines.
Rosehip, aster, marjoram, chamomile—
in summer, melliferous plants abound.
Bishop, saint: I sit in my kitchen,

my uncle's honey blooming in my tea.
I am lonely here, the winter is dark,
I know all that I love will pass away.
Help me to bear my fate,
you who came in praise of the miniature—
cells of wax, cells of notes
humming before the choristers,
each thorax of ink
soaring on its own black wings.

3 *Atlas*

Language has unmistakably made plain that memory
is not an instrument for exploring the past but its theater.
It is the medium of past experience, just as the earth
is the medium in which dead cities lie buried.

—Walter Benjamin, "A Berlin Chronicle"

Ultrasound

The transponder is slick and cold:
the nurse pushes it into me,
tiny vaginal submarine
flinging sound at my abdomen,
the part of me that Freud called
"the dark continent," and the shape
on the screen *is* black, a mesh net
pulsing with unseen, eyeless fish.
Yes, this cold probe's converting me
to image, and I'm glad it's not
Technicolor—red uterus,
pink ovaries, the tumor green.

I prefer to be dimly lit,
a decrepit chapel leading to
a crypt, a boulevard in Prague,
even the cave of a slipper,
spooky parabola for sound
to map, but blurred, approximate,
high-tech tea leaves that cast equal
parts of faith and doubt. I want to go
like that, though I'm writing this poem
on a screen, not unlike the screen
charting the awkward Italy
of my uterus: black letters,
black pulse, leading I'm not sure where.

Blue Paris

after the etching, "Little Funeral Procession in the Rain," 1879, by Félix Buhot

1

Paris has been pulled from a stone,
Paris has been greased and inked
until widows arise, blue as umbrellas
and spattered with the dull sheen of crow.
Someone's cranking the awning of the butcher shop
into oblivion. A woman is rushing home
to a jug of irises, delphinium china,
her wallpaper blooming. Will she make love
under a storm-colored comforter?
Will she drink ink in despair?
We creatures of electricity and jazz
can't know these things. We only see
what the artist sees. We only feel *our* blood
push through our own blue veins.

2

Consumptive himself, the artist wraps his throat in a grimy silk. ¶
The moribund one was no one he knew, but to judge from the horse
leading the cortege, a beast of more gristle than style, the unfortunate
was probably a pauper—some sclerotic clerk, or a fancier of low art
who'd drunk away his liver, or a widow who had spat her last into a
basin held by a sister of charity. ¶ Benedictions and a few *sous* to the
stallkeeper who lets artists roost under this awning when it rains in
Paris, clogged sewer of a city, on days when umbrellas weep, when
clouds press themselves to the mouths of chimneys as if to choke
back a cough, on days of damp shoes and ankles burning with chill,
when the Paris of bicycles, windowboxes, and crisp bread, suddenly
shivers in the clutch of ink.

From *The Indianapolis City Directory,* 1916: A Tally

Only one war memorial, two full pages of labor unions:
    Asbestos Workers of the World, Federation of Locomotive Engineers,
    the Musicians' Protective Association, and International Brotherhood
    of Book Binders

Fifty-two secret societies: the Odd Fellows, Order of Owl,
    Tribe of Ben-Hur, Masonic Temple (colored), Sisters
    of the Mysterious Tent (colored), Woodmen of the World,
    and the Improved Order of Red Men

Both a Prohibition Commission and two socialist parties,
    a Vacant Lots Cultivation Society
    and the *Deutscher Klub und Musik Verein*, Kurt Vonnegut, President

Schools included No. 3 Mary Turner Free Kindergarten (colored)
    and The Brooks Preparatory Academy for Boys,
    adjacent to the Home for Working Girls

An advertisement on every page:
    Fresh Beef, Veal, Mutton, and Pork
    Indianapolis Abattoir Company
    Endorsed by the Butchers Ladies Society

    Brevort Hotel, European Throughout,
    Rooms with Bath, $1.00 and Up

    Glide Bicycles, California Disappearing Bed Co.,
    Beatrice Du Valle, Lady Chiropractor

    Terre Haute Beer: We deliver to all parts of the city
    Try our Champagne Velvet, an ideal table beverage,
    or Radium, our effervescent, popular brand of the future

In Medias Res x 5

The beginning was never the beginning. The ending was never the end.

1

Hers was a poverty so genteel it didn't feel like poverty. Aniela Latarnik kept neat scrapbooks of her former concerts in Paris, New York, and Boca Raton. The Vietnamese takeout place delivered, and the Heinz office across the street—you know, the ones who pickle pickles—let her borrow their fax. She poured chocolate cereal into a china teacup to tempt the foreign visitor into renting her second story.

2

Trinh's mother had had an affair with a G.I. near Hue and now at 80, couldn't stop talking about it. Their studio apartment on Ziarnecka Street seemed to shrink a little each time her mother opened her mouth. The beige lacquered cabinets looked dirtier, and the tiny Polish refrigerator now reminded Trinh of one of those smelly Thai kerosene stoves, beside which the American, she was told, first "had" her mother.

3

The metro doors slid shut behind her with an airy puff. He wished he had a bottle to break or even a bag to stomp on. "Fuck you," she mouthed against the glass. Ten minutes later, at the mall, his phone rang in the pocket of his jeans. He hated that chiming cuckoo she'd made him choose. "Listen, jerkoff," she began, "I'm willing to talk if you are." He twisted the yin-yang keychain on his beltloop, and smiled.

4

Mrs. R had gone to the Church of St. Anne for a concert, only to discover the bishop was saying a Mass beforehand. Was she the only woman "of a certain age" in Warsaw who hated the bishop's self-important drawl? His sermon lasted 15, 20, no, 30 minutes! During the course of it, she watched the snow on her boots melt into a puddle by the kneeler. And when did her watchface get so scratched? How much longer, damn it, till they start the Russian hymns with Corelli as a second course?

5

"I feel like all I do now is go from funeral to funeral," Jacek said to the man who twenty years ago could have become his lover. But he would not cry in his presence. He would return to Krakow, to his Ukrainian wife. Only there, against her body smelling of bread and perfume, would he let his anguish out.

Breslau

In its 800 years of existence, the Silesian city of Breslau (in Polish, Wrocław) changed hands several times. In this poem, a German archaeology student from Breslau, though disgusted by Nazi propaganda that mythologizes the German past, becomes obsessed with preserving ordinary artifacts of daily life in the city. Ironically, after the war, when Breslau again becomes Wrocław, most traces of its German past are obliterated.

1928
You see everything in layers:
trees, cities, species, the sexuality
of the boy who shares your desk.
Sap rings, slivers of terra cotta, fossilized
insects with horned teeth, Marlene Dietrich in black
stockings and garter belt, Marlene sucking
on a long cigarette, spongy Marlene tissue
that summons blood to the penis.

1939
You slouch against the pillows
like an invalid. It doesn't help
that you received a first in Classics.
From the balcony opposite
you hear trumpets pointed
toward the distant Reichstag, toward the gaudy
Victory Angel whose wingspan is broad
as a Luftwaffe bomber's.
When the loudspeakers first crackle
with references to ancient Rome,
you can already picture
the enormous central mass
of the *Jahrhunderthalle*
crumbling into lacy ruin
like the great Colosseum.

1945

A hairless kitten licks your leg. Sometimes
you kick it to stop its senseless
Mühe, Mühe. You leave your bed only
after dark. By night, under the blacked out
starless sky, you bury things so people will know
the Breslau of your childhood. By day,
you catalogue everything in this room
like an archaeologist. Not just *saucer* and *transom*
but the way the rounded bottoms
of teacups fit, the oily aroma of coal wafting in.
Not just your mother's *eyeglasses* but the tiny scrolls
of nacre along the bridge. Not just *featherbed*
but the boy who kissed you over and over
in Hungarian.

Imagining Walter Benjamin, 1939

[In September] Benjamin was sent with many others to an internment camp at Nevers. It was a completely empty château, with no light and no beds. Benjamin slept at the foot of a spiral staircase. . . A survival market soon developed. Benjamin would offer lessons in philosophy to "advanced" pupils in exchange for three Gauloises or a button.

—*Roberto Calasso,* The Forty-Nine Steps

Denizen of libraries and bookstalls,
Jew who furnished his study with framed, bewildered saints:
I watch you shrink to the size of a briefcase,
your black satchel the only boulevard
where nothing is rationed, where umbrellas
and handkerchiefs still unfurl in peace,
and you can stroll, ecstatic and alone,
through blue arcades of ink.

Months before you slit your throat,
you founded a camp newspaper,
offered lessons in dialectics, and meditated,
as always, on the essence of objects.
Dear Herr Doktor Benjamin,
former collector of first editions,
poised like Saint Sebastian
before the arrows' flight:

I can picture the smooth wood button in your palm—
refugee from somebody's waistband,
its four hollow eyes untroubled by smoke
curling from the smooth white chimneys
of French cigarettes.

Woman at Streetcar Stop

St. Charles Line, New Orleans

Gone are the feathered masks of Mardi Gras,
gone, too, the Krewe of Zulu tossing coconuts
to revelers. It's June, unending month of sweat
which glues her hair like chicken down
to her forgotten neck. Her shirtwaist—shirred
brown jersey knit—conceals a bladder pad
and crinkly arms. She's maybe sixty-five,
her butt a flabby saddle no one wants
to grab. Twenty years before, I'll bet
her swell of ass commanded stares,
and earlier, those heavy hips shook babies free.
So what if assholes call her "hag" or "crone."
I'm forty-four. To me, she's harbinger,
wherever she's headed: grocery store or HMO
or church named for the saint
who sang Last Rites to victims of the plague.
I'm off to tour the Cities of the Dead,
but first I watch her haul herself aboard
the trolley car, calves sculpted still, purse smashed
against her chest. I'd guess she's sixty-five.
And when some stranger offers her his seat,
she settles in to ride and ride.

During the Sorties over Baghdad

A woman works with lace panels.
        Under and under again: that is the beauty
                of French seams. First to flatten with steam

back and forth back and forth.
        Then to stitch the unwavering rows
                the perfect parallels, all measures metric

all precise. To pinpoint the trajectory
        to plant the staccato thread under and under.
                This is the music of a thousand nights:

curtains scattered with trellises and roses
        scalloped along the valance and edges.
                Curtains fit for a window without flaw:

Eight glass polygons, caulked, soldered
        fringed with the January frost, overlooking
                a city that has never been bombed.

Cleveland, 1991

Meditation at the Gästehaus Mezcalero, Dresden

In this yellow room, old Odin—
"Spear-Thruster," the one who is "Glad of War"—

has shrunk to the size of a splinter, and in his place
there's Tlaloc, Aztec god of fertility and rain.

When I go out in this city twice destroyed by fire,
Tlaloc, you with your humid hands,

you who shelter souls struck by lightning,
wrap me in a poncho of cloud.

Show me this new Dresden in all its rivered splendor
and the city that was: copper domes melting,

maimed sandstone saints in Theaterplatz,
or opera-goers in velvet, aboard the night's last tram.

Lorgnettes in their pockets, still humming the chorus,
they are travelling toward a future without mirrors.

Requiem for the Buddhas of Bamiyan

If we gain something, it was there from the beginning.
If we lose something, it is hidden nearby.
                                        —*Ryokan*

Between the empire of China
            and the empire of Rome,
in an oasis along the Silk Road,

you heard pomegranates change hands
            in Latin and Farsi and Greek.
Chinese generals, Persian merchants,

inventors of gunpowder and algebra,
            fanciers of rhubarb and bronze:
all conducted their commerce

in your shadow: you
            who saw monasteries cut from mountains,
you who were sculpted out of sandstone,

who listened to the whispers of Christians;
            who welcomed Muslims and Manicheans,
disciples of Nestor and Zoroaster.

Leopards and lions rolled past you
            in their cages, actors
mimicked peacocks and parrots, travelers

who'd thirsted through the Taklamakan Desert
            gave thanks to plural gods.
You who survived Genghis Khan's cannon,

who saw the British retreat, then Soviets and Americans,
            you whom the Taliban ringed
with burning tires, blackening your face,

you with dynamite in your groin, you witness
            to starving farmers, to secret schools for girls:
for fourteen centuries you stood fast

still as Siddhartha
            on the night of his enlightenment,
as much a part of this valley as the wind.

Who will know you now by your absence,
            remembering your before?
When the night comes, who will know you?

When the ash falls, who will know you?
            After earthquakes and eclipses,
wherever there is fire,

how to feel you filling us and leaving us,
            abiding in the grottoes
of our breath?

Songs for a Belgrade Baker

With electricity cut by NATO bombs, she waits in candlelight for her customers.
—New York Times *photo caption, May 24, 1999*

Reportage

Her shoulders ache. In ten minutes they will wander in
from the cellars, wanting breakfast for the children,
a sandwich loaf, something crusty that would stand up
to soup. The line will curl through the dark shop.
They will point, choose, and their purchases she will tally
by hand. Later, there'll be a rock concert, a rally.
By then, if she's lucky, she'll be asleep under feathers,
dreaming of the tiny horns named for cuckolds and whether
they will lose their curl in the ovens, for the young ones,
deprived of Ninja Turtles, are hungry for these pointy buns.

Corporeal

This is my body, this is yours
The sour mother rising in the bowl
will bring forth fingers, horns, and plaits
O armpit of pumpernickel, groin of corn
give it to us black and blonde
Sink into the beds of our bellies
and grow us new bones

Folkloric

Offer it with salt to welcome a weary traveller
Sign each braid with a cross before baking
He who steps on a crumb will make the souls in limbo weep
Drop a slice on the floor—kiss it before eating
Salute the bride with a loaf, and she will be happy in bed

Antiphonal

Blessed are the Slovenes, for they are the cake-makers

Blessed are the Croats, for they excel at fish

Blessed the Macedonians, for their black wine gave birth to philosophy

Blessed, too, the Bosnians for the subtlety of their tongues—who else
would season veal with lemon and hibiscus?

Blessed the Herzegovinians, for their silver wine strengthens friendships

Blessed the Serbs, for their bean soup makes foreign clerics sweat

Blessed the Albanians for their love of cinnamon

And blessed are the olive trees and vineyards, goats and sheep,

for they serve both parable and table

Blessed are the mint and dill, for they are the peacemakers

And blessed the yeast and sponge, the sour-gray loaves, for they have
inherited the earth

Notes

page 7   "Warsaw Architect" is for Witek Gabryś.

page 11 The song cited on this page is my translation of a stanza from a 1920s cabaret number called "*Dymek z papierosa*" (literally, "Smoke from a Cigarette"). "Farce" is for Dr. Szymon Bojko.

page 16 "Fable" is dedicated to Józef Bierzało.

page 47 "Woman at Streetcar Stop" was inspired by a photograph by Jessica Jewell.

page 49 Alexander McKee's *Dresden 1945: The Devil's Tinderbox* (New York: Dutton, 1984) was of use to me in the writing of this poem. I also wish to thank the hospitable folks at the Gästehaus Mezcalero, an inn that is decorated with Aztec motifs, located in the Neustadt area of Dresden.

page 52 Lesley Chamberlain's *The Food and Cooking of Eastern Europe* (London, New York: Penguin, 1989) enriched the culinary catalogue in "Songs for a Belgrade Baker."